More than

Just

Monogamy

31 March 2009

Olney Central College
Olney, Illinois

Debbie Barry

Originally Written as
Debbie Palmer

2nd Edition

Published by:
Debbie Barry
2500 Mann Road, #248
Clarkston, Michigan 48346
USA

ISBN-13:   978-1546471271
ISBN-10:   1546471278

More Than Just
Monogamy

Donna is a middle-aged, white woman living in a small town in the mountains of western Virginia in the first half of the twenty-first century. She and her two sons attend a popular Christian church on Sundays and several times during the week. Her sons do well in the local public school, and she is active in both of their classes. To all appearances, Donna is a very ordinary mom, but there is more to her story. Donna shares household responsibilities with Bobbi. Donna and Bobbi are co-wives, and their husband, Lucas, is the father of all of their children. Because they live in the United States, where monogamy is mandated by law, Lucas is legally married only to Donna, but they all three share an agreement that Bobbi is also his wife. This arrangement works well for Donna and Bobbi, who share child rearing responsibilities and divide household responsibilities, and they present an appearance of solidarity. It is not an ideal situation, however, as Bobbi is sometimes jealous of the benefits Donna accrues from her legal marital status, and as Donna is sometimes jealous of Lucas's clear favoritism towards Bobbi's children, but the co-wives have learned to talk through their differences in the interests of maintaining the family's economic stability.

Donna, Bobbi, and Lucas live in the United States, where their family structure is looked on with scorn and disgust, and where Donna is often pitied by those who perceive Lucas as an unfaithful husband and Bobbi as an immoral mistress. They are judged by the prevailing Judeo-Christian view of marriage in this country.

However, although monogamy is the most common, and the best-favored, marriage form in the United States, and is the norm against which our culture measures the marriage forms of other cultures, it is not the only correct marriage form for humans worldwide. [1]

Roberta Lenkeit notes that "monogamy, the form of marriage in which one woman is married to one man, is the most common form of marriage around the world. It is not, however, the most preferred; monogamy is the ideal and preferred form of marriage in only eighty-one cultures out of a sample of four hundred cultures, according to a 1967 survey" (Lenkeit 152). In fact, a 1967 study by the anthropologist Murdock shows that "among the 849 human societies examined … the vast majority (83%) practiced polygyny, men having more than one wife; monogamy was characteristic of only 16% of the societies" (Hughes para. 13). With almost four times as many societies favoring polygyny as those that favor monogamy, it is clear that polygamy is the most viable marriage form for a very large part of the world's population, not monogamy. Unfortunately, the United States takes a more narrow-minded view of relationships than its international neighbors and attempts to force others to do the same by attaching negative connotations to any lifestyle choice that is more accepted than monogamy.

Many forms of marriage are practiced throughout the world, and they are generally divided into two categories: monogamy[2] and polygamy[3]. Monogamy is further divided into loose, patriarchal monogamy, which excuses or even condones men having extramarital relationships with other women, and strict monogamy, where there is no sexual concourse by either spouse with any other partner. In various parts of the world, very specific forms of monogamy are also practiced: levirate, or brother-in-law marriage[4]; sororate, or sister-in-law marriage[5]; same-sex marriage; and ghost marriage, which will be addressed later. Polygamy is divided into three categories: polygyny[6], polyandry[7], and group marriage, with two or more husbands and two or more wives in one marital group. In almost every culture there may be found examples of both monogamy and polygamy, regardless of the prevalent form for a particular culture, and even regardless of the laws, customs, and taboos of the culture. The only reason for this is that there is no one, absolutely correct form of marriage that works for every family in every culture, and each different marriage form is "correct" for those who choose to practice it.

Marriage, in its many forms, is an important factor in human relationships. Every society has some form of marriage (Lenkeit 151), which may confer status to one or more of the spouses, establish inheritance rights, create bonds between and among families and other social groups, provide for the economic security of the spouses, legitimize the children of a married couple, and fulfill religious or ceremonial requirements. Some marriages only fill some of these roles, other marriages fill other roles, but it is clear that marriage is important. It is dangerously myopic for Americans to view every marriage that is anything other than the exclusive, monogamous union of one man and one woman as wrong, and yet that is often what happens, resulting in stigmatization and ostracism of not only the parties involved, but also the children in the family. Rather than force everyone to conform to one standard, Americans need to recognize the diversity of cultures in the world, and to accept and value the uniqueness of other cultures, both inside and outside the borders of the United States.

In the United States, it is generally accepted that marriage is a sacred institution and that a marriage consists of one man and one woman who promise to be faithful to each other. This view of marriage continues to be held in American society despite the prevalence of divorce and cohabitation without marriage. Although "there is no constitutional requirement that marriage exist solely between a man and a woman" (Hamilton para. 20), "in order to preserve marriage as that of 'one man with one woman'… in 1890…the US government systematically led a criminal and economic assault on a religion and essentially at a point of a gun, forced its religious leaders to recant a core part of their religious beliefs" (Newman para. 8). This action on the part of the United States government underscores how strongly people feel about marriage, and to what lengths society is willing to go to preserve what it believes to be the best – indeed the only – way for families to exist.

What the United States government fails to realize, however, is that monogamy is not the only form of marriage in the world. Polygamy is common in cultures in Africa, India, and even North America. In many cultures, polygamy is the preferred way of life, and monogamy is seen as being unusual. Even in North America, polygamy is more common than most people realize, despite the laws which have been passed to prevent it. "Indeed, studies have found polygamy present in 78% of the world's cultures, including some Native American tribes. (While most are polygynists — with one man and multiple women — there are polyandrists in Nepal and Tibet in which one woman has multiple male spouses.) As many as 50,000 polygamists live in the United States" (Turley para. 9). The estimates of how many polygamists actually live in North America vary from source to source because polygamy is a crime and polygamous families usually prefer not to be identified too openly. Many families do continue to practice polygamy in the United States and Canada, however, indicating that monogamy is not as universally accepted as most politicians and religious leaders wish people to believe: "Polygyny is widely practiced in certain areas of the U.S. states of Utah and Arizona and the Canadian province of British Columbia among Fundamentalist Mormon denominations. Various individuals and groups estimate that many tens of thousands of adults -- up to 100,000 spouses -- are involved in polygynous relationships" (Robinson para. 11). Clearly, if so many individuals are willing to risk having legal action taken against them because they engage in polygamous marriages, there must be some merit in polygamy as a marriage form.

Unfortunately, the United States government has a long history of causing difficulties for families which practice polygamy, dating back to 1862 (Selick para. 9). The Morrill Act and the Edmunds Act, which were both enacted in the nineteenth century to suppress and eliminate polygamy in the Mormon Church, are examples of the United States government's attempt to mandate monogamy within its borders.

> In 1862, Congress enacted the Morrill Act, making bigamy a felony in order to stop Mormons from practicing polygamy. The Supreme Court upheld the law in Reynolds v. United States in 1879...In 1882 Congress passed the Edmunds Act making "bigamous cohabitation" a misdemeanor which, along with a jail sentence, would bar a person from serving

on a jury, voting, or holding public office. This led to 1,300 Mormon men being jailed and disenfranchised under the law in the 1880's. (Newman para. 6)

In the Supreme Court's 1879 decision,

the court refused to recognize polygamy as a legitimate religious practice, dismissing it…as "almost exclusively a feature of the life of Asiatic and African people."…the court declared polygamy to be "a blot on our civilization" and compared it to human sacrifice and "a return to barbarism."…the court found that the practice is "contrary to the spirit of Christianity and of the civilization which Christianity has produced in the Western World." (Turley para. 6)

These laws worked in opposition to the United States Bill of Rights, which states that "Congress shall make no law respecting an establishment of religion, or prohibiting the free exercise thereof" (Jordan 45). The Mormons, against whom the Morrill and Edmunds Acts were enacted, are a well-recognized religious group, and they are unable to openly practice polygamy, which is a part of their faith, because of the United States Supreme Court's insistence that Western civilization is based on Christianity.

If one recalls the scenario that opened this study, under the Edmunds Act of 1882, although Lucas is only legally married to Donna, it is necessary to note that Donna, Bobbi, and Lucas are a bigamous family, and bigamy is a form of polygamy. Donna, Bobbi, and Lucas are not Mormons; they live together because each woman is the mother of two of Lucas's four children and it is economically practical for Lucas to support one household instead of trying to support two separate households. Donna, Bobbi, and Lucas are not criminals, and they are not seeking to harm anyone by their way of life, but their behavior "is in their case a victimless crime—a mere offence against state fiat" (Selick para. 6), and is classified as criminal; they are in constant danger of being arrested for their attempts to provide a safe, stable, loving home for their children.

Although the laws of the United States forbid polygamy, "many people take the attitude that … polygamy should just be left alone as a matter between consenting adults" ("Polygamy a factor" para. 3). The Supreme Court's 2003 decision *Lawrence v. Texas*, in which the United States Supreme Court "ruled that governments cannot criminalize private activities by adults just because the majority considers them to be immoral" (Robinson para. 11), and "that extends to private, consensual sex acts - including sodomy[8], whether homosexual[9] or heterosexual[10] - that ensures that such acts cannot be criminally prosecuted" (Hamilton para. 14), "has probably given a boost to those favoring polygamous and polyamory living arrangements" (Robinson para. 11), and may be a step toward easing or eradicating the current marriage laws, which are established by the individual states, but which universally prohibit polygamy in the United States. In a time when personal freedoms are on the wane, this is a promising development for families. If the Supreme Court's ruling is interpreted correctly, it will overturn the Morrill and Edmunds Acts and reestablish a safe environment for American families to arrange themselves in whatever configurations work best for the individual families, without fear of government repercussions.

If one is willing to stop looking at marriages in the United States through prejudiced eyes and to consider the evidence that polygamous marriages are the successful, accepted norm in a number of other cultures worldwide, one will see that the United States does not set the standard for marriage practices, and even that polygamy continues to exist in the United States despite the laws against it. Examining several of these other cultures which allow and even encourage polygamy will illustrate the social and economic advantages which polygamous families enjoy when they are free to live according to family structures which best serve their individual needs.

Before discussing the advantages of non-monogamous marriages, it is necessary to address the arguments against them. As stated earlier, the loudest and most common arguments against polygamy and in favor of traditional monogamy – marriage between one man and one woman -- are based on religious convictions that monogamy is the only way two people can be married in the eyes of God, and an investigation of these beliefs will show that they are not universally held and that the arguments based on these beliefs lack rational, objective support, no matter how popular they may be, and that the sacred texts which are cited as proof that polygamy is wrong actually offer numerous examples of polygyny in the history of their faith. These convictions are most often Christian, and they are based on the teachings of the Holy Bible.

The first argument is that "God created Adam, and provided for him a single wife. He did not provide multiple wives for him, nor do we have any evidence that Adam ever had another wife. This original marriage relationship powerfully exposes God's intent for mankind's marriage relationships" ("Polygamy: What the

Bible says" para. 14). The problem with this is that the Holy Bible is the only source for the argument, and there are no historical records other than the Holy Bible that record mankind's history back to Adam, nor any that definitively state that Adam never had any other wife. This argument also assumes that everyone else in the world accepts the Holy Bible in the same way that Christians do, as the perfect and uncontestable word of God. Based on the vast number of different religions in the world, and on the variety of holy texts in print, it is clear that this assumption is untrue, and that the Holy Bible is no more than a work of mythology literature to many people around the world, having no authority over their thoughts, words, or actions.

Another argument offered by Christians against polygamy is: "Once a man has left his father and mother's authority and household to marry, he cannot leave that household again! This means that when a man first marries a woman, he does so upon leaving his parent's authority. If he were to subsequently marry another woman, he would not be leaving his parent's authority again, and thus would not fulfill the definition of marriage as outlined in Matthew 19 and Genesis 2:24[11]" ("Polygamy: What the Bible says" para. 13). This argument is also based solely on the Holy Bible, with the same difficulties that were mentioned for the first argument. This argument does not leave any option available for the widower or the widow to remarry, as the widower would not be leaving his parents' authority to do so, even though in I Corinthians 7:8-9 of the Holy Bible the Apostle Paul gives permission for the widow to marry: "I say therefore to the unmarried and widows, It is good for them if they abide even as I. But if they cannot contain, let them marry: for it is better to marry than to burn" (I Corinthians 7:8-9). When the source of an argument contradicts itself, as this source does, the argument itself cannot stand, and must be dismissed until a stronger support for the argument is found.

Continued study reveals that the Old Testament of the Holy Bible offers many examples of patriarchs of the Judeo-Christian faith practicing polygyny, which is ironic, since many of the patriarchs are celebrated and praised throughout Scripture as being faithful to God and living according to His will. However, in the eyes of modern society, these faithful, godly men would be looked upon with scorn and derision. Among the patriarchs are Elkanah[12], Jehoiada[13], Lamech[14], Esau[15], Jacob[16], Ashur[17], Gideon[18], King David[19], King Solomon[20], Rehoboam[21], and Abijah[22]. "Deuteronomy contains a rule for the division of property in polygamist marriages. Old Testament figures such as Abraham, David, Jacob and Solomon were all favored by God and were all polygamists. Solomon truly put the 'poly' to polygamy with 700 wives and 300 concubines" (Turley para. 8). Another argument against polygamy, which is refuted by the Holy Bible, is: "Rampant polygamy (and possibly all polygamy) was prohibited for kings, because it would cause them to turn from God... The Israelites should have reasoned that if this were true for kings, it would be true for others, hence polygamy was something they ought to avoid" ("Does God approve" para. 5). King Solomon is generally recognized as one of the most powerful kings of his period, and he is known best for his great wisdom. As noted above and described clearly in the Holy Bible, he also had seven hundred wives (1 Kings 11:3). King David is acclaimed as a great king who started out as a simple shepherd, saved his people when he slew Goliath with a sling and stone, and was later heralded as the head of the genealogical line from which Jesus Christ of Nazareth was born. In addition, the <u>Holy Bible</u> supports a man's right to take multiple wives when it says: "If he take him another [wife]; her food, her raiment, and her duty of marriage, shall he not diminish" (Exodus 21:10) and "Those that remain of him shall be buried in death: and his widows shall not weep" (Job 27:15). Clearly, if a woman's food, clothing, and status (duty of marriage) are not diminished by being taken as a man's additional wife, then their marriage is to be considered right and appropriate, because if their marriage was considered adulterous then the woman would be stoned for adultery. Similarly, if having multiple wives is considered to be wrong, then the women associated with a man are not his widows after his death; instead, they are his concubines, as concubinage[23] is common in Old Testament times. Religiously-accepted polygamy continues to exist in mainstream religions of the West today: "Martin Luther at one time accepted polygamy as a practical necessity. Polygamy is still present among Jews in Israel, Yemen and the Mediterranean" (Turley para. 8). In addition to Judeo-Christian examples of polygamy, "Mohammed had 10 wives, though the Koran limits multiple wives to four" (Turley para. 8).

There are arguments against polygamy which are not based on religious beliefs or sacred texts. One of these is the argument that "polygyny … is a violation of women's rights" (Anyolo para. 6). Against this is Celestine Obi's research among the Igbo in Nigeria and other tribes around the world. "Igbo women, do not detest the husband's marrying other wives. As for the Igbo, so also the Kaggirs, the Ashanti, the New Guineans, and the Eskimos. An Akikuyu East African woman gave the following message to the women of Europe: 'Tell them two things, one is that we never marry anyone we do not want to, and the other is that we like our husband to have as many wives as possible'" (Obi para. 39). The Akikuyu woman's opinion is quite clear: she does not feel that her rights are being violated, nor that she is in any way being exploited or mistreated. In fact, in some cultures, including that of the Igbo, "polygyny is widely regarded as a moral virtue; to support as many fellow human beings as possible is not only a mark of wealth but a form of philanthropy" (Obi para. 39). In these cultures, polygyny is seen as saving women from loneliness and misery by giving the women husbands and the opportunity to have social and economic stability and to produce babies.

An additional argument against polygamy is that "underage girls have been coerced into polygamist marriages" (Turley para. 12). This arises from the polygynous cults which have appeared in the news from time to time, in which a single charismatic male leader takes a large number of very young wives and keeps all of them, with their resultant children, in a fortified compound with nearly Draconian rules for the women and children. Turley goes on to say that "There are indeed such cases. However, banning polygamy is no more a solution to child abuse than banning marriage would be a solution to spousal abuse. The country has laws to punish pedophiles and there is no religious exception to those laws" (Turley para. 12). Child abuse occurs throughout the United States, and around the world, but it is not caused by monogamy, polygamy, or any other marriage form. Polygamy has become a scapegoat for heinous acts against young girls, but that is not the basis of polygamy, and so should not be the basis for laws which are enacted out of fear or ignorance.

One last argument against polygamy which needs to be addressed is the idea that monogamous marriage favors natural selection among humans. "In fact, out of all mating systems, monogamy is arguably the one most conducive to natural selection, since it curbs 'marrying up' and condemns most low-status individuals to eventual genetic death (their places being taken by downwardly mobile descendants of higher-status individuals)" (P. Frost para. 3). What Frost fails to recognize is that low-status individuals all over the world marry and produce offspring every day of every year. There is no shortage of such individuals and families in the world, and they may be seen in every major city, small town, and tribal village. In past times in Europe, these were the peasantry. In every age they represent the bulk of the workforce for low-level jobs that higher-status individuals will not lower themselves to perform. These are the people who fill our public aid offices, who occupy our shelters and low-income housing, and whose children grow up to study technical trades and follow in their parents' footsteps. Monogamy does not keep the poor or the disadvantaged from marrying; rather, monogamy prevents some low-status individuals from moving up in the world as second or third spouses to higher-status men and women.

Far from interfering with natural selection, polygamy has been shown to have health benefits for individuals who practice it. "New research suggests that men from polygamous cultures outlive those from monogamous ones" (Callaway para. 1) and "it seems that fathering more kids with more wives leads to increased male longevity" (Callaway para. 17). If polygamy increases longevity, then it appears that polygamy, not monogamy, favors natural selection by allowing polygamous men to survive longer than monogamous men. Additionally, since "the male is programmed to fertilize as many females as possible, while the female aims to seduce as many males as possible so that she may choose the best of all" (M. Frost para. 2), it is only reasonable that polygamous men and women should enjoy better health as they act with the natural urges and impulses of their bodies, instead of expending a great deal of mental, emotional, and physical energy fighting against nature. Chris Wilson, an evolutionary anthropologist at Cornell University in Ithaca, New York, says: 'It doesn't surprise me that men in those societies live longer than men in monogamous societies, where they become widowed and have nobody to care for them' (Callaway para. 19). Rather than cutting low-status individuals out of the breeding pool through monogamy, "polygamy was a way by which the carriers of the best 'genetic material' could sooner or later couple and procreate better offspring after a number of trials and errors" (M. Frost para. 7). With more opportunities to create strong, healthy children to continue the race, polygamous cultures allow natural selection, instead of human selection, to do its work.

While it might seem that the arguments against polygamy are many and persuasive, it is important to look at each one carefully, and not to get caught up in an emotional whirlwind of rhetoric. As has been shown above, each argument against polygamy has a clear, rational answer which shows that polygamy is not the evil that Americans imagine and fear. Polygamy is instead a natural response to mankind's need for personal status, security of family life, a clear pattern for the accumulation of wealth and its inheritance, personal and societal health, and a reduction in societal violence, as will be shown below.

In many cultures, polygamy – specifically, polygyny – confers status on the husband who is able to attract, win, and support multiple wives. At the same time, being married confers status on the wives, who are often defined in their cultures by their roles as wives and mothers.

> Polygyny dignifies a woman, and marriage is a status symbol. It prevents immorality in the community and controls diseases. Polygyny is a strategy to ensure that almost all women get married in order to wipe out all evils that accompany the existence of a large population of eligible but unmarried women. It also reduces the large number of men's extramarital affairs. Polygyny offers more children for the security of family life without the stigma of being born out of wedlock. (Anyolo para. 14)

This description from a study of the Ovambadja in the Okalongo area of Namibia indicates that polygyny represents many positive things for the people who practice it. For the Ovambadja, polygyny creates a stable, workable family structure, in which the women are protected, the men have no reason to seek companionship outside of marriage, and the children have a secure future with clear rules of inheritance. Many other cultures have the same experiences of polygyny and polyandry: their marriage practices give status to the men (or the women, in the case of polyandry), dignify the women, and ensure the legitimacy and security of the children and the future.

Polygyny grants status to the husband because it tells his society that he is important or powerful enough to attract multiple wives, strong enough to keep them with him, and wealthy enough to provide for his wives and their children. In many cultures, the man also has to pay a bride price to the woman's family for each of his wives, and his ability to do so increases his status. This feature of polygyny is found in cultures around the world: "Among Alaskan Eskimos, among New Guinea mountain Papuans, and among relatively untouched South American Indians, polygamy is widespread, and it is the individual with leadership qualities who has the greatest chance to have several wives" (P. Frost para. 1). Among the North American Eskimos, as well, "it has observed that whereas each husband married one wife, a man of fair means could marry two or more to make himself socially important" (Obi para. 31). This also carries over to segments of the monogamous culture of the United States, in which strong, powerful, wealthy men often support mistresses as a way of displaying their power to their associates. In other cultures, this is called concubinage, and has been an accepted practice since before the Christian era, but in the United States, with its requirements of monogamy, this practice is viewed as immoral, decadent, and wrong. If polygyny was an accepted practice in the United States, men like these could marry their women and accrue legitimate social status, instead of the illicit status they now bear among their peers.

As observed among the Ovambadja, polygyny is recognized as helping to reduce immoral behavior among those who adopt this family structure. As Newman notes in his discussion of polygamy and same-sex marriages, "equating polygamy with degeneracy[24] raises a few issues" (Newman para. 2). Newman discusses the legal actions that were taken against the Mormons in the nineteenth century and states that "however you feel about polygamy, the historical assault on it within the United States should shame everyone" (Newman para. 5). In many cultures outside the United States, polygamy in its various forms is seen not as degeneracy, but as a legitimate means of preventing immoral behavior. "Polygyny well understood and as it exists among Igbos is as distinct from promiscuity[25] as darkness is from daylight" (Obi para. 36). While polygyny is, by the strictest definition of the word, a form of promiscuity, in that the husband does have multiple sexual partners, it is not promiscuity in the moral sense, in which it is understood to be illicitly having more than one sexual partner. In polygyny, the man's wives are his legitimate, licit sexual partners.

In cultures which practice polygamy, the marital form ensures the stability of the family. Again recalling the scenario referenced at the start this paper, Donna, Bobbi, and Lucas live as they do so that all of their children will grow up with their father, so that Donna and Bobbi will each have less work to do by sharing household responsibilities, and so that Lucas can afford to provide a better standard of life for his family by not having to support two separate households. In British Columbia, Canada, there is a community called Bountiful in which this same family stability is the norm. In Bountiful, "a group of breakaways from the Mormon church are practicing polygamy" (Selick para. 4). It does not surprise too many people to hear about polygamy in Africa, Asia, and the Middle East, as Americans tend to think of those places as primitive and backward, despite the fact that mankind had its start in the Middle East and the cultures of Africa and Asia were ancient and thriving before the European Middle Ages. However, despite this historical fact, it is more troubling for many Americans to learn that polygamous families are flourishing in North America, because American prejudices say that polygamy is counter to the ways of Western civilization, but families such as Donna, Bobbi, and Lucas's and communities such as Bountiful indicate that polygamy can be a viable way of life for North American families. In her article in the August 2005 issue of <u>Canadian Lawyer</u>, Selick says:

> Although sharing a husband with another woman wouldn't be my cup of tea, I don't understand why our lawmakers insists that polygamy be outlawed. Some of the Bountiful women declare unambiguously that they enjoy their way of life, that they are there voluntarily, and that they don't want their "plural marriages" broken up by criminal charges. They cite the sharing of household chores and the caring relationship with their co-wives as among the advantages. (Selick para. 5)

As in the United States, it is illegal in Canada for three or more adults to live together and have sexual activity between any one adult and any two or more other adults, singly or otherwise, and that behavior is considered to be polygamous, regardless of marriage or its absence. However, these laws fail to consider that the women of Bountiful are content with their life, and are there of their own free will. Their polygynous marriages provide them with advantages which contribute to the stability of their personal and family lives.

The stability associated with polygamy is not limited to North America. In Nepal, "polyandrous households appear to have more continuity and stability than extended families made up of monogamous couples" ("Nepali Marriage and Family" para. 2). In Nepal, monogamous husbands, with or without their wives, often have to seek employment outside the village or even outside the country in order to earn enough money to support their families. Although polygyny is practiced in Nepal, "a number of Tibetan-speaking people, such as the Nyinba, Sherpa, and Baragaonli, practice variant forms of fraternal polyandry" ("Nepali Marriage and Family" para. 1). In those families, where one woman has two or more husbands who are brothers to each other, there are fewer tensions regarding status and inheritance, and the husbands are more likely to be able to support their families without having to leave their village, so the family structure is more stable than for the monogamous families of Nepal.

Among the Igbo of Nigeria, polygyny is also important to the social status of women. "Inu nwunye (marriage) states Dr. Basden, 'has a foremost place in Igbo social economy...a childless woman is regarded as a monstrosity...in fact the birth of the child gives her the title of wife, before this time she may be said to be a wife only in anticipation'" (Obi paras. 1-3). A woman of the Igbo must marry in order to have children and to fulfill her proper role in her society. In order that every woman may have a husband and family, "just as it is the custom that among the Lango people of Uganda, there is no limit, so also among the Igbos there is none either. It is not uncommon to find a man with 5 to 10 wives or sometimes even more...where it is difficult to obtain a husband, polygyny creates a situation that will make it possible for many more women to be absorbed into the married state" (Obi paras. 35-36). A man with five, ten, or more wives also accrues increased status from his ability to provide for so many wives and children, although the wives and children also contribute to the family's economic success, as discussed below.

Along with conferring status on the men and dignity on the women who practice it, polygamy strengthens a family's economic status and provides clear lines of inheritance. Brian Schwimmer defines marriage as: "a relationship established between a woman and one or more other persons, which provides that a child born to the woman under circumstances not prohibited by the rules of the relationship, is accorded full birth-status rights common to normal members of his society or social stratum" (Schwimmer, "Defining Marriage" para. 5). The other persons may be a husband and co-wives, or they may be two or more co-husbands, but the goal is the same: to provide full birth-status rights, or legitimacy, to the woman's children. "Polygyny produces wealth not only for the man, but for the whole family – which is one of the reasons why there is no poverty in societies that practise polygyny" (Anyolo para. 15). When there are no unwed mothers and illegitimate children to draw on a society's resources, everyone experiences improved economic stability. In a polygynous society, every woman is able to marry, even if there are fewer men than women, and her children are recognized as being legitimate. When more individuals are contributing to a family's income, or to its production of food and other goods, the entire family profits from the increase. In addition, polygamy may be practiced if a spouse is unable to produce or raise children or if a spouse becomes incapacitated and cannot continue to perform the functions of a spouse, so that the remaining spouse does not have to shoulder all of the responsibilities of the family alone.

Polygamy exists in the United States for more than just religious or economic reasons. Sometimes, when a spouse becomes incapacitated due to trauma or illness, the healthy spouse will seek a new partner to fill the void the impaired spouse leaves in the family. Often, the new partner not only takes the original spouse's place in the family, but also provides care for the co-spouse. An example of this sort of family arrangement is the family of Dennis and Julie, who live in central Vermont in the last decade of the twentieth century. They have been married for fifteen years, and Julie has been raising Dennis's son from a previous marriage. Thirteen years ago, Julie developed brain cancer which had to be surgically removed, taking with it a small portion of her frontal lobe. Three years ago, when Dennis's son was 16 years old and Julie had regressed to a mental and emotional age of 6 years old, Dennis met Diane and asked her to move in with the family. Diane was aware that Dennis and Julie were married, but she was also aware that Julie was no longer capable of fulfilling even the most basic roles of a wife and mother because of her condition. Also because of Julie's condition, Dennis felt that he could not in good conscience divorce her or cease to provide for her. Diane is now the de facto wife in Dennis's household. She takes care of Dennis, his son, and Julie. Diane has taken on the role of step-mother to Dennis's son, and has seen him through his formative teen years. Because Dennis and his family live in the United States, he and Diane are unable to marry, but they share physical and financial responsibility for their home and family.

By becoming Julie's caregiver and co-wife, Diane has eased the burden of living with a handicapped spouse for Dennis. Her presence in the home has allowed Dennis to work without having to worry about Julie's welfare while he is away from home each day. She has obviated the need for Dennis to spend a significant portion of his earnings on hiring outside caregivers for Julie and a housekeeper to take Julie's place in the daily upkeep of the home. The family structure has secured the family's economic stability. [26]

Just as Dennis, Julie, and Diane experience improved domestic conditions in their home from the interaction of co-spouses who can share the burdens of life, families throughout the world, such as the Dongria Kondh of India, enjoy the benefits of shared responsibilities and experiences, as well as increased economic security, through their practice of polygyny. "The Dongria family is normally simple nuclear family consisting of father, mother and their unmarried children... is patrilocal[27] and patrilineal[28]...and polygynous...the woman is more diligent and hard working in comparison to their male counterparts. She does all sorts of household work...she is treated as an economic asset to the family" (Kanungo paras. 3-4). Among the Dongria Kondh, the more wives a man has, the more economic stability and wealth his family has. His wives represent a labor force for the family, as do their children as they become old enough to do work in the home and the fields. In addition, a "girl child is preferred over boy child" (Kanungo para. 4) because a man will collect a bride price from the family of each daughter's husband before she is allowed to marry, so a man with many daughters will accrue a large amount of money from their marriages, but a man with many sons will have to pay a bride price for each of his sons to marry. This is the reverse of the practice in monogamous cultures of Europe and North America, where a man had to pay a dowry for each of his daughters to marry, but was paid a dowry by the parents of each of his sons' wives.

The Nayar of India is a matrilineal[29] society which practices an unusual form of polyandry. Among the Nayar, "sambandan involved a man having a 'visiting husband' relationship with a woman. While such relationships were considered to be marriages by the woman's family, especially when they occurred with males of higher subcastes or castes, the males tended to view the relationships as concubinage. Traditionally Nayar women were allowed to have more than one 'visiting husband' either simultaneously or serially" ("Nayar Marriage and Family" para. 1). To properly understand and discuss this visiting husband arrangement, it is necessary to include a more detailed account of Nayar marriage practices:

> Before puberty a Nayar woman was formally married to a man from a family with whom her family had a special relationship. The two were together for a few days, and then the marriage ended. The woman usually never saw this husband again, though she and her future children might mourn when this man died. After this marriage the woman was considered an adult and was free to take up to a dozen lovers. Each lover was part of a formal relationship approved by her family, and the man was required to give the woman gifts three times a year until the relationship ended. The "visiting

husbands" as they were called, spent the night with a woman, leaving a shield or sword outside of her door so that other men with whom she had a similar relationship knew that another "husband" was visiting that night. The visiting husbands never resided with a woman, did not have any economic obligation to her, and came and went as their military duties dictated. When a child was conceived, one of the visiting husbands established the child's legitimacy by claiming paternity and presenting gifts to the woman and to the midwife who delivered the child. He had no further economic responsibilities for this child, though he might take a social interest in it. The child lived with and was the economic responsibility of the mother's group. (Lenkeit 151-152)

The Nayar system exists because of the warlike nature of the Nayar. It is usual for all of the men to be away from their villages for the majority of their adult lives in military service. Since Nayar men are not available to settle in villages and establish families in any of the usual patterns – monogamous, polygynous, or polyandrous – the Nayar contrived the system of visiting husbands. In this system, it is not important which man genetically fathers which child, but only that one of the mother's husbands claims paternity for each child; the children's inheritance is through the maternal line, from mother to daughter, and the mother's maternal female relatives ensure economic provision and cultural security for all of the children born to their group. Although "the 'visiting husband' had...no responsibility for any children he might sire" ("Nayar Marriage and Family" para. 2) the men of the Nayar are not excused from providing economic support for the women. "His main responsibilities were for his sister's children" ("Nayar Marriage and Family" para. 2). Thus, the men of the Nayar provide for their mothers and sisters, and not for their wives and children, who are in turn provided for by the wives' brothers and sons.

In certain patrilineal cultures special arrangements have been made to provide for the inheritance of men who have no male heirs. Among these arrangements are woman-to-woman marriage, ghost marriage, Nwunye Nhachi or "wife of the village", and Nwunye Nkuchi or "inherited wife".

Woman-to-woman marriage is not lesbian marriage, and the women do not engage in sexual activities with each other. It is practiced by the Zulu women of the Neur and the Nandi in Africa. Among the Neur, "a rich and influential Zulu woman may marry another woman by giving marriage cattle for her, and she is the pater of her wife's children begotten by some male kinsman of the female husband" (Obi para. 26). By having the wife mate with the brothers and male cousins of the female husband, the children born of the marriage do, indeed, carry the female husband's genes, and the children are true heirs of the female husband.

Woman-to-woman marriage for the purpose of producing heirs and securing inheritances is also important to the Nandi of Africa who "practice patrilineal descent...the most common option for a woman without an heir is woman-to-woman marriage, in which the woman with no male heir becomes a husband to another woman...children born to this couple are considered heirs of the female husband. In other words, when the 'wife' has a child, that child is considered to be the heir of the female husband" (Lenkeit 203-204). When the Nandi practice woman-to-woman marriage, the female husband takes on the male gender roles in the family, and the wife continues to perform the female gender roles. The spouses do not live together, however, so that the wife is able to take male lovers in an effort to become pregnant. It is understood that, regardless of who biologically fathers the wife's children, they are the heirs of the female husband. The female husband typically does not take lovers of either gender while in a woman-to-woman marriage.

Ghost marriage is practiced among the Igbo of Nigeria and among tribes in East and Central Africa. "'Ghost marriage'…consists in a woman being married to the name of a man who died unmarried so that his line need not die out. Consequently, children born of this marriage should bear the name of this unmarried dead man" (Obi paras. 27-28). The wife of the dead man takes male lovers in an effort to provide heirs for her husband, and, as with woman-to-woman marriage, it is understood that any children born to the wife are the heirs of her dead husband, regardless of who actually fathers the children.

Nwunye Nhachi or "wife of the village" is another marriage form used by the Igbo of Nigeria to secure lines of inheritance for men who die without male heirs. "When a man dies without a male issue, one of his daughters stays back, selects lovers with whom she cohabits to beget children on behalf of her dead father" (Obi para. 29). In this case, the daughter is theoretically married to her father after his death, and does not marry another man. Any children born to this daughter-wife are her heirs – and by extension, her siblings.

Nwunye Nkuchi or "inherited wife" is also practiced by the Igbo, and is something of the reverse of Nwunye Nhachi. "A man by this practice takes over his dead father's wife or dead brother's wife where there is no heir, or male issue or if the heir is a minor" (Obi para. 27). In this case, the husband provides economic support for the widows, and future heirs born to the widow-wives are the heirs of their dead husbands because their marriages continue after their husbands' deaths.

In many societies where polygamy is the prevalent form of marriage, not only does polygamy provide economic stability and secure inheritances but there is a reduction in the occurrences of domestic violence as compared to societies where monogamy is the prevalent form of marriage. In her study of the Ovambadja of Namibia, Prisca Anyolo notes that "at present, violence against women in Namibia is more prevalent through domestic violence, followed by rape and the killing of women...but none of the cases of violence has so far been attributed to the practice of polygyny...such violence and social discrimination against women is prevalent in almost all 13 Regions of the country, and even more so in Regions where polygyny does not exist" (Anyolo paras. 8, 13). Although violence against women does exist in areas where polygyny is practiced, it is clear that there is less violence in these areas, and as with the counter-argument about child abuse which is presented earlier in this discussion, one cannot assume or expect that violence against women will summarily stop if any relationship other than monogamy was allowed, any more than one may assume that violence against women will summarily increase if all relationships other than monogamy are prohibited.

Violence is not limited to the atrocities of beatings, rape, and murder. Violence in a family also includes jealousies among family members and drawing distinctions between and among individuals to establish the relative value of the individuals. In these cases, as well, the occurrence of violence is reduced in polygynous families. "As a rule, the jealousy of co-wives is not the characteristic of Igbo polygyny" (Obi para. 36). Like Donna and Bobbi, Igbo co-wives are able to work out the small differences which inevitably exist between and among people who live and work in close contact with one another, so any jealousies which arise are quickly disposed of. Unlike monogamous wives whose husbands conduct extramarital affairs without the approval of their wives, Igbo wives do not need to be jealous of their co-wives, because they all live together by their own will and share equally in their husband's time, attention, and resources.

Culture exists in part to create systems for living which promote the best interests of the members of the group and which secure the orderly existence of the society. Marriage forms a part of this system of orderly existence. "At the time polygyny was established as the legal form of marriage" in Liberia, "the ratio of women to men in Africa was about 10 to 1" (Nyanseor para. 8). An African woman's role is to marry and to produce children, not unlike the traditional expectation for Western women, who are still seen primarily as wives and mothers despite the 'women's movement' and 'equal rights'. An African woman's secondary role is to keep the house and to help her husband produce a living for her family. With a ratio of ten women to each man, polygyny is the only way most women are able to fulfill their role in their society. The Liberian leaders recognize this concern and the "elders, including women, decided to come up with a marriage system that would address this problem. Their aim at the time was to provide a balance and equal distribution of social, material, security and economic benefits to both women and men" (Nyanseor para. 8). Polygyny is the solution the Liberian elders devised, and it fulfills the aim of providing that balance. When Christian settlers from America arrive in Liberia, they bring the idea of monogamy with them, but the Christian settlers do not practice true monogamy. Instead, they practice a new form of marriage, which becomes known as Chrismonopoly. "Chrismonopoly…is an arrangement in which a male settler is married to his monogamous or Christian wife and at the same time is engaged in polygynous relationship with 'native African Liberian women'" (Nyanseor para. 14). The settlers do not view their own behavior as polygyny, although that is what it is. They do not treat their Liberian wives and children equally with the way they treat their American wives and children, unlike the polygynous Liberian husbands, who treat their wives and children equally. In the settlers' families, "a distinction was made as to who were 'inside or outside children'" (Nyanseor para. 18), which causes dissention and strife for the settlers, but "this was never the case in a polygynous relationship" (Nyanseor para. 18). By treating his wives and children equally, a polygynous Liberian husband avoids the family violence which his monogamous Christian neighbor creates in his own family.

Among the Eskimo of North America, jealousy among co-wives is nearly non-existent. A wife who is unable to bear children "pays for a new life on behalf of her husband, or she provides him with the necessary funds for a new marriage, with a view to raising children for her husband by proxy as we may put it" (Obi para. 25). The first wife welcomes the new co-wife and accepts the co-wife's children as part of the family. In an interview about why her husband takes another wife, an Eskimo woman reports that 'I asked him myself, for I am tired of bearing children' (Obi para. 36). For this woman, having a co-wife means she is relieved of some of the pressure and stress of her wifely duties; the first wife benefits from her polygynous lifestyle, as does the co-wife, who can fulfill her role of wife and mother, but also has stability and protection because of the family structure.

A form of polygamy which is less familiar than polygyny and polyandry is group marriage. Most Americans associate group marriage with the communes of the 1960's, and some of those were, in fact, group marriages. Group marriage is not about orgies[30] or sexual free-for-alls, however, and it is not polyamorous[31] wife-swapping; it is true marriage involving at least two husbands and at least two wives. A notable occurrence of group marriage is "the Kaingang in Brazil, where 8 percent of the population practiced this marriage form during historic times. The remainder of the population practiced monogamy (60 percent), polygyny (18 percent), or polyandry (14 percent). Obviously there are diverse ideas about marriage among the Kaingang" (Lenkeit 155). Although group marriage is not the most prevalent marriage form among the Kaingang, eight percent of the population represents a significant number of people engaged in group marriage. An additional example of group marriage is the Gilyak tribe of the island of Sakhalin, in which "every Gilyak has the rights of a husband in regard to the wives of his brothers and to the sisters of his wife; at any rate, the exercise of these rights is not regarded as impermissible" (Engels, "Appendix. A Recently Discovered Case of Group Marriage" para. 3). Among the Gilyak, the entire tribe is one large, group marriage, with each adult the parent of each child, regardless of which two adults produced the child. This arrangement is very similar to the punaluan marriage custom of Hawaii, in which

> a number of sisters, own or collateral (first, second or more remote cousins) were the common wives of their common husbands, from among whom, however, their own brothers were excluded; these husbands now no longer called themselves brothers, for they were no longer necessarily brothers, but punalua -- that is, intimate companion, or partner. Similarly, a line of own or collateral brothers had a number of women, not their sisters, as common wives, and these wives called one another punalua. (Engels, "The Punaluan Family" para. 2)

Among the Hawaiians, unlike the Gilyaks, a spouse's siblings of the opposite sex could not be included in the spouse's group marriage. Siblings, in this case, refer to cousins as well as to conventional siblings.

One additional marriage form exists which is not a form of polygamy, but is also not traditional monogamy. This is same-sex marriages other than those discussed above as means of securing inheritances. This is, instead, homosexual marriage between two men or two women who love each other and who wish to bind themselves together with a formal commitment of marriage. Same-sex marriage is not a new concept, despite its frequent appearance in the media in the last decade. "Data demonstrate that same-sex unions, including marriage, have been recognized in the histories of many cultures – Greek, Roman, and pre-Columbian Native American cultures, as well as various African cultures and numerous cultures in Asia and the Pacific" (Lenkeit 156). Same-sex marriage is not often spoken of openly in Western society because it is alien to people who believe in strict monogamy, and who have grown up being taught that the Bible forbids homosexuality[32]. Many cultures, however, do not recognize the <u>Holy Bible</u> as the true law, or even as anything more than a work of mythological fiction, and so those cultures are not guided by the <u>Holy Bible</u>. In the United States, only Connecticut, Massachusetts, New Jersey, New Mexico, New York, Rhode Island, and Vermont allow same-sex marriages; each of the other 43 states has a law which bans same-sex marriage, although New Hampshire, New Jersey, and Oregon allow same-sex civil unions distinct from marriage, and Alaska, California, the District of Columbia, Hawaii, Maine, and Washington allow certain protections for same-sex couples (Stritof).

While marriage should be a matter between and among the spouses, in the United States marriage has become a sore point of politics. For almost a century and a half, the United States government has legislated what constitutes a marriage and who may marry whom. Many fear that the increased tolerance for same-sex marriage in the United States may open the way for polygamous marriage to become a legally accepted fact of American life and fear the collapse of their own systems of morals and ethics if monogamy ceases to be the only legal and accepted marriage form in the United States. What these people fail to recognize is that, with the legalization – or at least tacit legalization by not banning – same-sex marriages in seven states, and with an estimated 100,000 individuals living polygamous lifestyles in the United States, monogamy has already ceased to be the only accepted form of marriage in the United States. "Just as it is said that no system of government, is necessarily the best, so also it can be said that all things being equal, no system of marriage is necessarily the best" (Obi para. 37). Throughout the world, and even within the cultural bastion of the United States, this comparison has proven to be true; no one system of marriage emerges from the fray as the one, single, definitive best form of marriage for every family and every situation. Each form has its merits, and each form has its drawbacks, and each individual, couple, and group needs to have the freedom to openly choose which form is best for that particular situation.

With the many personal and social benefits experienced by polygamous families, group families, same-sex families, and monogamous families, it behooves Americans to learn tolerance for ways of life which are different from mainstream American culture. As editorial columnist Jonathan Turley writes in the October 3, 2004, issue of USA Today,

> I personally detest polygamy. Yet if we yield to our impulse and single out one hated minority, the First Amendment becomes little more than hype and we become little more than hypocrites. For my part, I would rather have a neighbor with different spouses than a country with different standards for its citizens.
>
> I know I can educate my three sons about the importance of monogamy, but

> hypocrisy can leave a more lasting
> impression. (Turley paras. 16-17)

Each person is capable of living a full, satisfying life without needing to control what is going on in the bedrooms next door, down the street, across the state, or on the other side of the world. It is up to each parent or parental group to raise its children with a set of values which allow the children not only to make good choices for their own relationships, but also to respect and honor the relationship choices which are made by others. Far from monogamy being the only correct marriage form in the world, it is only one of many forms, each of which is "correct" for those who choose it as their way of life.

End Notes:

1. Donna, Bobbi, and Lucas are real people, and the situation described is real. Their names have been changed to protect their privacy.
2. "The state or custom of being married to one person at a time" ("Monogamy").
3. "Marriage in which a spouse of either sex may have more than one mate at the same time" ("Polygamy").
4. "A marriage custom in which a widow marries her deceased husband's brother" (Lenkeit G-5).
5. A marriage custom in which a widower marries a sister of his deceased wife" (Lenkeit G-8).
6. "The state or practice of having more than one wife or female mate at a time" ("Polygyny").
7. "The state or practice of having more than one husband or male mate at one time" ("Polyandry").
8. "Anal or oral copulation with a member of the same or opposite sex; also: copulation with an animal" ("Sodomy").
9. "Of, relating to, or involving sexual intercourse between persons of the same sex" ("Homosexual").
10. "Of, relating to, or involving sexual intercourse between individuals of opposite sex" ("Heterosexual").
11. "And he answered and said unto them, 'Have ye not read, that he which made them at the beginning made them male and female, And said, For this cause shall a man leave father

and mother, and shall cleave to his wife: and they twain shall be one flesh? Wherefore they are no more twain, but one flesh. What therefore God hath joined together, let not man put asunder'" (Matthew 20:4-6).

"Therefore shall a man leave his father and his mother, and shall cleave unto his wife: and they shall be one flesh" (Genesis 2:24).

12. "And he had two wives; the name of the one [was] Hannah, and the name of the other Peninnah: and Peninnah had children, but Hannah had no children" (1 Samuel 1:2).

13. "And Jehoiada took for him two wives; and he begat sons and daughters" (2 Chronicles 24:3).

14. "And Lamech took unto him two wives: the name of the one [was] Adah, and the name of the other Zillah" (Genesis 4:19).

15. "And Esau was forty years old when he took to wife Judith the daughter of Beeri the Hittite, and Bashemath the daughter of Elon the Hittite" (Genesis 26:34).

"Then went Esau unto Ishmael, and took unto the wives which he had Mahalath the daughter of Ishmael Abraham's son, the sister of Nebajoth, to be his wife" (Genesis 28:9).

16. "And he went in also unto Rachel, and he loved also Rachel more than Leah, and served with him yet seven other years" (Genesis 29:30).

17. "And Ashur the father of Tekoa had two wives, Helah and Naarah" (1 Chronicles 4:5).

18. "And Gideon had threescore and ten sons of his body begotten: for he had many wives" (Judges 8:30).

19. "And when David heard that Nabal was dead, he said, Blessed be the Lord, that hath pleaded the cause of my reproach from the hand of Nabal, and hath kept his servant from evil: for the Lord hath returned the wickedness of Nabal upon his own head. And David sent and communed with Abigail, to take her to him to wife. And when the servants of David were come to Abigail to Carmel, they spake unto her, saying, David sent us unto thee, to take thee to him to wife. And she arose, and bowed herself on her face to the earth, and said, Behold, let thine handmaid be a servant to wash the feet of the servants of my lord. And Abigail hasted, and arose, and rode upon an ass, with five damsels of hers that went after her; and she went after the messengers of David, and became his wife. David also took Ahinoam of Jezreel; and they were also both of them his wives. But Saul had given Michal his daughter, David's wife, to Phalti the son of Laish, which was of Galim" (1 Samuel 25:39-44).

"And unto David were born sons in Hebron: and his firstborn was Amnon, of Ahinoam the Jezreelitess; and his second, Chileab, of Abigail the wife of Nabal the Carmelite; and the third, Absolom the son of Maacah the daughter of Talmai king of Geshur; and the fourth, Adonijah the son of Haggith; and the fifth, Shephatiah the son of

Abital; and the sixth, Ithream, by Eglah David's wife. These were born to David in Hebron" (2 Samuel 3:2-5).

"And David took him more concubines and wives out of Jerusalem, after he was come from Hebron: and there were yet sons and daughters born to David" (2 Samuel 5:13).

"And David took more wives at Jerusalem: and David begat more sons and daughters" (1 Chronicles 14:3).

20. "But king Solomon loved many strange women, together with the daughter of Pharaoh, women of the Moabites, Ammonites, Edomites, Zidonians, [and] Hittites; of the nations [concerning] which the LORD said unto the children of Israel, Ye shall not go in to them, neither shall they come in unto you: [for] surely they will turn away your heart after their gods: Solomon clave unto these in love. And he had seven hundred wives, princesses, and three hundred concubines: and his wives turned away his heart. For it came to pass, when Solomon was old, [that] his wives turned away his heart after other gods: and his heart was not perfect with the LORD his God, as [was] the heart of David his father. For Solomon went after Ashtoreth the goddess of the Zidonians, and after Milcom the abomination of the Ammonites. And Solomon did evil in the sight of the LORD, and went not fully after the LORD, as [did] David his father. Then did Solomon build an high place for Chemosh, the abomination of Moab, in the hill that [is] before Jerusalem,

and for Molech, the abomination of the children of Ammon. And likewise did he for all his strange wives, which burnt incense and sacrificed unto their gods" (1 Kings 11:1-8).

21. "And Rehoboam took him Mahalath the daughter of Jerimoth the son of David to wife, [and] Abihail the daughter of Eliab the son of Jesse; which bare him children; Jeush, and Shamariah, and Zaham. And after her he took Maachah the daughter of Absalom; which bare him Abijah, and Attai, and Ziza, and Shelomith. And Rehoboam loved Maachah the daughter of Absalom above all his wives and his concubines: (for he took eighteen wives, and threescore concubines; and begat twenty and eight sons, and threescore daughters.) And Rehoboam made Abijah the son of Maachah the chief, [to be] ruler among his brethren: for [he thought] to make him king. And he dealt wisely, and dispersed of all his children throughout all the countries of Judah and Benjamin, unto every fenced city: and he gave them victual in abundance. And he desired many wives" (2 Chronicles 11:18-23).

22. "But Abijah waxed mighty, and married fourteen wives, and begat twenty and two sons, and sixteen daughters" (2 Chronicles 13:21).

23. "Cohabitation of persons not legally married" ("Concubinage").

24. "Sexual perversion" ("Degeneracy")

25. "Promiscuous sexual behavior" ("Promiscuity").

"Promiscuous - not restricted to one sexual partner" ("Promiscuous").

26. Dennis, Julie, and Diane are real people, and the situation described is real. Their names have been changed to protect their privacy.

27. "Of or relating to residence with a husband's kin group or clan" ("Patrilocal").

28. "Relating to, based on, or tracing ancestral descent through the paternal line" ("Patrilineal").

29. "Tracing descent through the maternal line" ("Matrilineal").

30. "A sexual encounter involving many people; also: an excessive sexual indulgence" ("Orgy").

31. "The state or practice of having more than one open romantic relationship at a time" ("Polyamory").

32. "Thou shalt not lie with mankind, as with womankind: it is abomination" (Leviticus 18:22).

Works Cited:

1. Anyolo, Prisca. "Polygyny among the Ovambadja: A female perspective." 4 Feb 2009 <http://www.kas.de/upload/auslandshomepages/namibia/Women_Custom/anyolo.pdf>.

2. Callaway, Ewen. "Polygamy is the key to a long life." 19 Aug 2008. New Scientist. 5 Feb 2009 <http://www.newscientist.com/article/dn14564-polygamy-is-the-key-to-a-long-life.html?DCMP=ILC-hmts&nsref=news2_head_dn14564>.

3. "Concubinage". 2009. Merriam-Webster Online Dictionary. Merriam-Webster Online. 13 Mar 2009 <http://www.merriam-webster.com/dictionary/concubinage>.

4. "Degeneracy". 2009. Merriam-Webster Online Dictionary. Merriam-Webster Online. 13 Mar 2009 <http://www.merriam-webster.com/dictionary/degeneracy>.

5. "Does God approve of polygamy?" Rational Christianity: Christian Apologetics. 20 Feb 2009 <http://www.rationalchristianity.net/polygamy.html>.

6. Engels, Frederick. "Appendix. A Recently Discovered Case of Group Marriage." Origins of the   Family, Private Property, and the State. 17 Mar 2009 <http://www.marxists.org/archive/marx/works/1884/origin-family/appen.htm>.

7. —. "The Punaluan Family." Origins of the Family, Private Property, and the State. 17 Mar 2009 <http://www.marxists.org/archive/marx/works/1884/origin-family/ch02b.htm>.

8. Frost, Martin. "Monogamous marriage ceases to be acceptable form of sexual and family relations." 8 Dec 2006. 5 Feb 2009 <http://www.martinfrost.ws/htmlfiles/dec2006/mono_poly.html>.

9. Frost, Peter. "Polygyny and human evolution." 18 Feb 2008. Evo and Proud. 4 Feb 2009 <http://evoandproud.blogspot.com/2008/02/polygyny-and-human-evolution.html>.

10. Hamilton, Marci. "The Marriage Debate and Polygamy." 29 Jul 2004. 20 Feb 2009 <http://writ.news.findlaw.com/hamilton/20040729.html>.

11. "Heterosexual". 2009. Merriam-Webster Online Dictionary. Merriam-Webster Online. 13 Mar 2009 <http://www.merriam-webster.com/dictionary/heterosexual>.

12. Holy Bible, The. Trans. King James Version. Nashville, TN: Holman Bible Publishers, 1979.

13. "Homosexual". 2009. Merriam-Webster Online Dictionary. Merriam-Webster Online. 13 Mar 2009 <http://www.merriam-webster.com/dictionary/homosexual>.

14. Hughes, James J., Ph.D. "Monogamy as a Prisoners Dilemma: Non-Monogamy as a Collective   Action Problem." Dec 1990. 4 Feb 2009 <http://www.changesurfer.com/Acad/Monogamy/Mono.html>.

15. Jordan, Terry L. U.S. Constitution and Fascinating Facts About It, The. Naperville: Oak Hill Publishing Company, 2008.

16. Kanungo, Akshaya K., M.A., M.Phil. "Problems In Educating Tribal Children: The Dongria Kondh

Experience." 23 Sep 2005. 4 Feb 2009
<http://www.anthroglobe.info/docs/EDUCATIN
G-TRIBAL-CHILDREN-DONGRIA-
KONDH.htm>.

17. Lenkeit, Roberta Edwards. <u>Introducing Cultural
Anthropology.</u> New York: McGraw-Hill, 2009.

18. "Matrilineal". 2009. <u>Merriam-Webster Online
Dictionary.</u> Merriam-Webster Online. 5 Feb 2009
<http://www.merriam-
webster.com/dictionary/matrilineal>.

19. "Monogamy". 2009. <u>Merriam-Webster Online
Dictionary.</u> Merriam-Webster Online. 5 Feb 2009
<http://www.merriam-
webster.com/dictionary/monogamy>.

20. "Nayar Marriage and Family." 2008. <u>World
Culture Encyclopedia.</u> 4 Feb 2009
<http://www.everyculture.com/South-Asia/Nayar-
Marriage-and-Family.html>.

21. "Nepali Marriage and Family." 2008. <u>World
Culture Encyclopedia.</u> 4 Feb 2009
<http://www.everyculture.com/South-
Asia/Nepali-Marriage-and-Family.html>.

22. Newman, Nathan. "Why Gay Marriage is Like
Polygamy." 15 Mar 2004. <u>Progressive Populist.</u>
20 Feb 2009
<http://www.nathannewman.org/archives/003169.
shtml>.

23. Nyanseor, Siahyonkron. "Polygyny (Polygamy) Is
Already A Practice." 4 Feb 2009
<http://www.theperspective.org/polygyny.html>.

24. Obi, Celestine A. "Marriage Among The Igbo Of
Nigeria." <u>ATR Special Topics.</u> 4 Feb 2009
<http://www.afrikaworld.net/afrel/igbo-
marriage.htm>.

25. "Orgy." 2009. <u>Merriam-Webster Online Dictionary.</u> Merriam-Webster Online. 13 Mar 2009 <http://www.merriam-webster.com/dictionary/orgy>.

26. "Patrilineal." 2009. <u>Dictionary.com.</u> Merriam-Webster Online. 21 Feb 2009 <http://dictionary.reference.com/browse/patrilineal>.

27. "Patrilocal." 2009. <u>Dictionary.com.</u> 21 Feb 2009 <http://dictionary.reference.com/browse/patrilocal>.

28. "Polyamory." 2009. <u>Merriam-Webster Online Dictionary.</u> Merriam-Webster Online. 13 Mar 2009 <http://www.merriam-webster.com/dictionary/polyamory>.

29. "Polyandry". 2009. <u>Merriam-Webster Online Dictionary.</u> Merriam-Webster Online. 5 Feb 2009 <http://www.merriam-webster.com/dictionary/polyandry>.

30. "Polygamy". 2009. <u>Merriam-Webster Online Dictionary.</u> Merriam-Webster Online. 5 Feb 2009 <http://www.merriam-webster.com/dictionary/polygamy>.

31. "Polygamy a factor in marriage debates." 13 Mar 2006. <u>Religion Newswriters Foundation.</u> 20 Feb 2009 <http://www.religionlink.org/tip_040329b.php>.

32. "Polygamy: What the Bible says". 19 Jul 2006. 20 Feb 2009 <http://www.eadshome.com/polygamy.htm>.

33. "Polygyny". 2009. <u>Merriam-Webster Online Dictionary.</u> Merriam-Webster Online. 5 Feb 2009 <http://www.merriam-webster.com/dictionary/polygyny>.

34. "Promiscuity". 2009. <u>Merriam-Webster Online Dictionary.</u> Merriam-Webster Online. 13 Mar 2009 <http://www.merriam-webster.com/dictionary/promiscuity>.
35. "Promiscuous". 2009. <u>Merriam-Webster Online Dictionary.</u> Merriam-Webster Online. 13 Mar 2009 <http://www.merriam-webster.com/dictionary/promiscuous>.
36. Robinson, B.A. "SAME-SEX MARRIAGE AND POLYGAMY." 22 Feb 2005. <u>Ontario Consultants on Religious Tolerance.</u> 20 Feb 2009 <http://www.religioustolerance.org/ssmpoly.htm>
37. Schwimmer, Brian. "Defining Marriage." Sep 2003. 4 Feb 2009 <http://www.umanitoba.ca/faculties/arts/anthropology/tutor/marriage/defining.html>.
38. Selick, Karen. "Polygamy--Two Rights Shouldn't Make a Wrong." 2005. 20 Feb 2009 <http://www.karenselick.com/CL0508.html>.
39. Stritof, Sheri and Bob. "Same Sex Marriage License Laws." 2009. <u>About.com: Marriage.</u> 17 Mar 2009 <http://marriage.about.com/cs/marriagelicenses/a/samesexcomp.htm>.
40. "Sodomy". 2009. <u>Merriam-Webster Online Dictionary.</u> Merriam-Webster Online. 13 Mar 2009 <http://www.merriam-webster.com/dictionary/sodomy>.
41. Turley, Jonathan. "Polygamy laws expose our own hypocrisy." 3 Oct 2004. <u>USA Today.</u> 20 Feb 2009 <http://www.usatoday.com/news/opinion/columnist/2004-10-03-turley_x.htm>.

About This Book

This book was my final research paper for Freshman Composition and Analysis, in 2009, at Olney Central College, in Olney, Illinois. My professor was a truly delightful woman named Kelly Payne, who went out of her way to make sure that any student willing to learn would learn, and any student willing to put in the work needed to excel would excel. She challenged her students to be their best, and to do their best, and she did not accept half-measures.

This assignment was simple in concept, but not in execution. It was to choose a topic that would be considered controversial, with some restrictions to avoid over-used topics, and to research the topic. The research would inform the thesis, rather than conforming to a pre-conceived thesis. The final paper would be at least ten pages long, if I remember correctly, and would references at least ten sources, again trusting to my memory for the number. With the required MLA formatting, my final paper was 30 pages, with five pages of end notes, and four pages of works cited.

I have written many papers since completing this assignment, but this remains my favorite work. Although my personal religious views make me a firm monogamist, exploring the various polygamist cultures that still exist and succeed in the world was a fascinating experience. I am pleased to offer this alternative world-view to my readers.

Clarkston, Michigan
May, 2017

About the Author

 Debbie Barry lives with her husband in southeastern Michigan with their two cats, Mister and Goblin. They enjoy exploring history through French and Indian War re-enactment and through medieval re-enactment in the Society for Creative Anachronism (SCA). Debbie grew up in southwestern Vermont, where she heard and collected many family stories that she enjoys retelling as historical fiction for young audiences, and as family and local history for genealogists, as well as memory stories of her own life.

Debbie graduated summa cum laude with a B.A. in dual majors of social sciences with an education concentration and of English in 2013. She is on hiatus from pursuing her master's degree in linguistics, specializing in teaching English as a second language (TESOL), at Oakland University, in Rochester, Michigan, as a result of going blind and battling long-term illness.

Debbie went blind suddenly, without obvious cause, on December 15, 2014, at the age of 45. Her family, friends, and doctors expected her to give in to the darkness and become bitter and angry. Instead, Debbie chose to adopt a positive attitude, even when she felt anything but positive, and to find as much light as possible in her life. She wrote an autobiographical account of her first full year of living in the twilight semi-vision of blindness to share her experience with others; it was also therapy to help her face the darkness.

Before going blind, Debbie was an avid, even voracious, reader. She enjoyed drawing in many traditional media and painting in acrylic, gouache, and watercolor. She enjoyed sewing, crocheting, needlepoint, embroidery, beadwork, spinning, and weaving. Since going blind, Debbie has turned to audio books from Audible.com, BARD Talking Books Library, and on CDs. She crochets blankets and crochets scraves for charity. She makes paper beads to make rosaries for the missions. She has recently begun exploring how she can resume drawing and painting with the limitations of her diminished vision.

Debbie is an active member of the Daughters of the American Revolution (DAR) and the Society for Creative Anachronism (SCA). She is a past member of the LEO Club, the Lions Club, the Civil Air Patrol (CAP), the Girl Scouts, the Explorer Scouts, and the Order of the Eastern Star (OES), as well as various academic and social groups in high school, college, and graduate school. She is a member of the National Honor Society, Phi Theta Kappa, and the Golden Key Honor Sciety. She likes to be active.

Find out more about Debbie on LinkedIn:
http://www.linkedin.com/pub/debbie-barry/34/331419/

Find Debbie's Amazon Author Page at:
https://www.amazon.com/author/debbiebarry

Follow and Like Debbie's Facebook Author Page at:
https://www.facebook.com/authordebbiebarry/?ref=book marks

Shop Debbie's My Zazzle Store for clothing and gift items featuring Debbie's original artwork at:
http://www.zazzle.com/dkpalmer*

V I C E

IN ITS

PROPER SHAPE;

OR, THE

Wonderful and Melancholy

TRANSFORMATION

OF SEVERAL

NAUGHTY MASTERS AND MISSES

INTO THOSE

Contemptible Animals which they most
resemble in Disposition.

Printed for the Benefit of all GOOD Boys
and Girls.

THE FIRST *WORCESTER* EDITION.

PRINTED at WORCESTER, *Massachusetts,*
BY ISAIAH THOMAS,
Sold at his Bookstore, and by THOMAS
and ANDREWS in BOSTON.
MDCCLXXXIX.

More Books by the Author

Memoirs:
- Child of the Shire
- Child of the Shire (2nd Edition)
- Thirteen Days to Darkness

Books for Young Learners:
- Around the Color Wheel
- Colors and Numbers
- Five Green Speckled Frogs

Stories for Children:
- Bobcat in the Pantry
- Born in the Blizzard and Freshet
- The Collected Nursery Rhymes of Our Childhood (Comp. & Ed.)
- Expressing the Trunk
- Gramp's Bear Story
- Grandfather Singing Lark's Stories
- When Mary Fell Down the Well
- Writing Competition

History and Genealogy:
- Family History of Deborah K. Fletcher
- Grandma Fletcher's Scrapbooks
- Nana's Stories
- Property Deeds and other Legal Documents of the Fletcher and Townsend Families
- Property Deeds and other Legal Documents of the Fletcher and Townsend Families, 2nd Edition with Digital Scans
- The Red Notebook

- The Red Notebook, 2nd Edition with Digital Scans
- Zoa Fletcher's Photos
- Zoa Has Her Way

Linguistics:
- Acquisition of Morphology and Syntax in Children
- Examining Arabic and English Stops and Vowels
- Language Production and Language Perception: Development in Children Aged 1   to 5 Years
- Picturing The First Writing
- Serving ESL Clients in the Writing Center
- The Impact of Native Arabic on English Writing as a Second Language

Art and Writing:
- A Journey Through My College Papers: Undergraduate Series
- Debbie's Vision in Art, Volumes   1-4
- Debbie's Writing
- The Heart's Vision
- The Heart's Vision in Color
- Tommy Thumb's Song-Book

Other Topics:
- Advantages of Brain-Based Learning Environments
- African Americans in Post-Civil War America
- American Students Are Crippled   By Cultural Diversity Education
- Analyzing *The Yellow Wallpaper*

- Examining Gender in A Doll House
- Identity Within and Without
- Indifferent Universe
- Loss
- Nature in Early American Literature
- Religion and Myth in English Poetry
- Responsibility to a Broader   Humanity
- Speech Codes in Education
- Symbolic Serpents
- The Evil of Grendel

As Editor:
- Books by
  Father Frederick R. Engdahl, Jr.:
  - Prayers and Meditations
  - Blessing of the Season
  - In Midwinter
  - Lenten Journey